Superfoods for Exam Success

THE AUSTRALIAN Women's Weekly

contents

Studying for exams or preparing for a presentation or interview can be a stressful business. When you've got other things on your mind, it's tempting to skimp on food or snack on all the wrong things. With this compilation of recipes, you'll be able to feed both the brain and the body with the minimum fuss.

Pamela Clark
Food Director

However rushed you are, always find the time to eat breakfast. A bowl of cereal or a slice of toast, a glass of fruit juice or a smoothie will set you up for the day and provide the energy needed to stay physically and mentally alert.

pancetta and eggs

preparation time 5 minutes **cooking time** 10 minutes **serves** 2

4 slices pancetta (60g)

1 green onion, chopped coarsely

2 eggs

2 thick slices white bread

1 Preheat oven to moderately hot (200°C/180°C fan-forced). Grease two holes of 6-hole (¹/₃-cup/80ml) muffin pan.

2 Line each of the prepared holes with two slices of pancetta, overlapping to form cup shape. Divide onion among pancetta cups; break one egg into each pancetta cup.

3 Bake, uncovered, about 10 minutes or until eggs are just cooked and pancetta is crisp around edges. Remove from pan carefully. Serve on toasted bread.

PER SERVING 10.4g fat; 965kJ (231 cal)

breakfast

untoasted muesli

preparation time 10 minutes **serves** 6

2 cups (180g) rolled oats

½ cup (35g) processed bran

1 tablespoon sunflower seed kernels

⅓ cup (55g) sultanas

¼ cup (35g) finely chopped dried apricots

½ cup (80g) finely chopped seeded dried dates

3 cups (750ml) low-fat milk

½ cup (140g) low-fat yogurt

1 Combine oats, bran, seed kernels and dried fruit in large bowl.

2 Divide muesli and milk among serving bowls. Top with yogurt.

TIPS You can use fruit juice, such as apple juice, instead of the milk, if you prefer. Store leftover muesli in an airtight container for up to two weeks.

PER SERVING 4.1g fat; 1132kJ (270 cal)

bruschetta with strawberry, banana and ricotta

preparation time 15 minutes **cooking time** 10 minutes **serves** 4

½ loaf ciabatta (220g)

200g low-fat ricotta

2 tablespoons honey

1 teaspoon finely grated orange rind

¼ teaspoon ground cinnamon

125g strawberries, sliced thickly

1 small banana (130g), sliced thinly

2 tablespoons brown sugar

1 Trim end from bread; cut into eight slices.

2 Beat cheese, honey, rind and cinnamon in small bowl with electric mixer until smooth.

3 Combine strawberries, banana and sugar in small frying pan; stir gently over low heat until sugar dissolves.

4 Meanwhile, toast bread slices until lightly browned both sides. Spread with cheese mixture, divide among plates; top with strawberry mixture.

PER SERVING 5.8g fat; 1208kJ (289 cal)

breakfast with the lot

preparation time 10 minutes **cooking time** 25 minutes **serves** 4

2 large egg tomatoes (180g), quartered

4 eggs

4 slices multigrain bread

60g sliced ham

50g baby spinach leaves

1   Preheat oven to hot (220°C/200°C fan-forced). Line oven tray with baking paper.

2   Place tomato, cut-side up, on prepared tray; roast, uncovered, about 25 minutes or until softened and lightly browned.

3   Meanwhile, place enough water in a large shallow non-stick frying pan to come halfway up the side; bring to a boil. Break eggs, one at a time, into small bowl, sliding each into pan; allow water to return to a boil. Cover pan, turn off heat; stand about 4 minutes or until a light film of egg white has set over each yolk.

4   Toast bread slices until lightly browned both sides.

5   Using an egg slide, remove eggs, one at a time, from pan; place egg, still on slide, on absorbent-paper-lined saucer to blot up any poaching liquid. Serve toast topped with ham, spinach, egg then tomato.

PER SERVING 7g fat; 680kJ (160 cal)

cheesy egg-white omelette with herbs

preparation time 25 minutes **cooking time** 20 minutes **serves** 2

6 egg whites

2 green onions, chopped finely

2 tablespoons finely chopped fresh chives

¼ cup finely chopped fresh flat-leaf parsley

½ cup (65g) grated pizza cheese

1   Preheat grill.

2   Beat half the egg whites in small bowl with electric mixer until soft peaks form; fold in half of the combined onion and herbs.

3   Pour mixture into heated lightly oiled medium non-stick frying pan; cook, uncovered, over low heat until omelette is just browned lightly on the bottom.

4   Sprinkle half the cheese on half the omelette. Place pan under grill until cheese begins to melt and omelette sets; fold omelette over to completely cover cheese. Carefully slide onto serving plate; cover to keep warm.

5   Repeat process with remaining egg whites, onion and herb mixture, and cheese.

PER SERVING 7.9g fat; 620kJ (148 cal)

chocolate hazelnut croissants

preparation time 15 minutes **cooking time** 15 minutes **makes** 8

2 sheets ready-rolled puff pastry

⅓ cup (110g) chocolate hazelnut spread

30g dark chocolate, grated finely

25g butter, melted

1 tablespoon icing sugar mixture

1 Preheat oven to hot (220°C/200°C fan-forced). Lightly grease two oven trays.

2 Cut pastry sheets diagonally to make four triangles. Spread chocolate hazelnut spread over triangles, leaving a 1cm border; sprinkle each evenly with chocolate.

3 Roll triangles, starting at one wide end; place 3cm apart on prepared trays with the tips tucked under and the ends slightly curved in to form crescent shape. Brush croissants with melted butter.

4 Bake, uncovered, about 12 minutes or until croissants are browned lightly and cooked through. Sieve croissants with icing sugar mixture; serve warm or at room temperature.

TIP Leftover croissants can be stored in an airtight container for up to four days. Eat cold or reheat in microwave oven on HIGH (100%) for 20 seconds.

PER CROISSANT 17.7g fat; 1153kJ (275 cal)

baked eggs with ham and cheese

preparation time 10 minutes **cooking time** 10 minutes **serves** 2

25g shaved ham, chopped coarsely

1 green onion, chopped finely

2 eggs

2 tablespoons coarsely grated cheddar

1 Preheat oven to moderate (180°C/160°C fan-forced). Grease two ½-cup (125ml) ovenproof dishes.

2 Divide ham and onion among dishes. Break eggs, one at a time, into small bowl, carefully sliding egg from bowl over ham and onion into each dish. Sprinkle dishes with equal amounts of cheese.

3 Place dishes on oven tray; bake, uncovered, about 10 minutes or until yolk is just set. Serve with toast, if desired.

TIP By breaking the eggs into a small bowl first, you will be able to discard any bad egg without ruining the other ingredients in the dish.

PER SERVING 9.1g fat; 540kJ (129 cal)

breakfast

Muesli is a high-fibre cereal mix that typically contains wheat flakes, oats, bran, dried fruit and nuts. Oats help to lower cholesterol levels due to their high fibre content and, along with dried fruits, ward off mid-morning energy dips.

peach muesli

preparation time 25 minutes (plus refrigeration time) **serves** 4

2 cups (220g) natural muesli

1⅓ cups (330ml) apple juice

¾ cup (200g) low-fat yogurt

1¼ cups (185g) dried peaches, chopped coarsely

2 tablespoons honey

¾ cup (180ml) low-fat milk

1 medium pear (230g), peeled, grated

1 large peach (220g), cut into wedges

¼ cup (15g) toasted shredded coconut

1 Combine muesli, juice, yogurt, dried peach, honey and milk in large bowl. Cover; refrigerate overnight.

2 Stir pear into muesli mixture; serve topped with peach wedges and sprinkled with coconut.

TIP Dried and fresh peach can be replaced with any fruits such as apricots, berries or apple.

PER SERVING 8.6g fat; 2002kJ (479 cal)

porridge with yogurt and honey

preparation time 5 minutes **cooking time** 5 minutes **serves** 1

¾ cup (180ml) hot water

⅓ cup (30g) rolled oats

2 tablespoons milk

2 tablespoons vanilla yogurt

1 teaspoon honey

1 Combine the water and oats in small saucepan over medium heat; cook, stirring, about 5 minutes or until porridge is thick and creamy. Stir in milk. Serve topped with yogurt and honey.

TIP To prepare in a microwave oven, combine the water and oats in small microwave-safe bowl, cover; cook on HIGH (100%) for 2 minutes, pause and stir. Cook again, covered, on HIGH (100%) for 1½ minutes, pause and stir. Cover; stand 5 minutes, then stir in milk.

PER SERVING 4.5g fat; 801kJ (191 cal)

buckwheat pancakes with lemon cream

preparation time 10 minutes **cooking time** 10 minutes **serves** 4

½ cup (75g) buckwheat flour

¼ cup (35g) wholemeal self-raising flour

1½ teaspoons baking powder

½ teaspoon ground cinnamon

2 egg whites

¾ cup (180ml) milk

1 tablespoon lemon juice

2 tablespoons maple syrup

2 teaspoons coarsely grated lemon rind

LEMON CREAM

⅓ cup (80g) low-fat sour cream

1 teaspoon finely grated lemon rind

1 teaspoon caster sugar

1 Sift flours, baking powder and cinnamon into medium bowl; gradually whisk in combined egg white, milk, juice and syrup.

2 Pour ¼ cup batter into heated lightly greased small non-stick frying pan; cook about 2 minutes or until bubbles appear on surface. Turn pancake; cook until lightly browned on other side. Remove from pan; cover to keep warm. Repeat with remaining batter. Serve with lemon cream; top with rind.

LEMON CREAM Place ingredients in small bowl; stir until combined.

PER SERVING 6.3g fat; 903kJ (216 cal)

breakfast

15

vegetable juice

preparation time 10 minutes
makes 1 cup (250ml)

1 small beetroot (100g), chopped coarsely

1 small carrot (70g), chopped coarsely

1 cup firmly packed baby spinach leaves

½ cup (125ml) water

1   Push beetroot, carrot and spinach through juice extractor. Dilute with the water; stir to combine.

PER 250ml 0.2g fat; 230kJ (55 cal)

drinks

orange, apple, carrot and ginger juice

preparation time 10 minutes
makes 1 cup (250ml)

1 medium orange (240g), peeled, chopped coarsely

1 large apple (200g), cored, chopped coarsely

1 medium carrot (120g), chopped coarsely

2cm piece fresh ginger (10g), peeled

1   Push ingredients through juice extractor. Stir to combine.

PER 250ml 0.6g fat; 903kJ (216 cal)

raspberry cranberry crush

preparation time 5 minutes
makes 2 cups (500ml)

1½ cups (375ml) cranberry juice

1 cup (150g) frozen raspberries

2 tablespoons lemon juice

1   Blend or process ingredients until smooth.

TIP   Add a little icing sugar, if you prefer this drink sweeter.

PER 250ml 0.2g fat; 543kJ (130 cal)

Fruit is an excellent source of natural sugars and provides energy fast. Dark fruits are high in anti-oxidants which help to heal the body and protect against diseases. Citrus fruits are high in vitamin C. Ginger may help reduce the symptoms of migraine and tension headaches.

pineapple orange frappé

preparation time 10 minutes
makes 2 cups (500ml)

½ medium pineapple (625g), chopped coarsely

¼ cup (60ml) orange juice

1½ cups crushed ice

2 teaspoons finely grated orange rind

1   Blend pineapple and orange juice, in batches, until smooth.

2   Pour into large jug with crushed ice and rind; stir to combine.

PER 250ml 0.2g fat; 309kJ (74 cal)

spiced iced coffee milkshake

preparation time 10 minutes (plus standing time)
makes 1 litre (4 cups)

¼ cup (20g) ground espresso coffee

¾ cup (180ml) boiling water

2 cardamom pods, bruised

¼ teaspoon ground cinnamon

1 tablespoon brown sugar

3 scoops (375ml) low-fat vanilla ice-cream

2½ cups (625ml) low-fat milk

1 Place coffee then the boiling water in coffee plunger; stand 2 minutes before plunging. Pour coffee into small heatproof bowl with cardamom, cinnamon and sugar; stir to dissolve sugar then stand 10 minutes to cool.

2 Strain coffee mixture through fine sieve into blender or processor; process with ice-cream and milk until mixture is smooth.

PER 250ml 1.6g fat; 510kJ (122 cal)

mixed berry smoothie

preparation time 5 minutes
makes 2 cups (500ml)

100ml frozen low-fat strawberry yogurt, softened slightly

⅓ cup (50g) frozen mixed berries

1 cup (250ml) low-fat milk

1 Blend or process all ingredients, in batches, until smooth.

PER 250ml 3.6g fat; 724kJ (173 cal)

spiced chai tea

preparation time 10 minutes (plus standing time)
makes 2 cups (500ml)

1 cinnamon stick

½ teaspoon cardamom pods, bruised

½ teaspoon fennel seeds

¼ teaspoon whole cloves

½ teaspoon ground ginger

¼ teaspoon ground nutmeg

¼ cup firmly packed fresh mint leaves

2 tea bags

1 cup (250ml) milk

1 cup (250ml) water

white sugar

1 Combine spices, mint and teabags in teapot or heatproof jug. Bring combined milk and water to a boil, pour over spice mixture; stand 10 minutes.
2 Sweeten with a little sugar, if desired. Just before serving, strain.

PER 250ml 5g fat; 418kJ (100 cal)

Dairy products, including the low-fat varieties, are an excellent source of protein and calcium. Protein is essential for the body's growth and repair. Calcium helps regulate blood pressure and maintains healthy teeth and bones.

banana soy smoothie

preparation time 5 minutes
makes 2 cups (500ml)

1 cup (250ml) low-fat soy milk

1 medium ripe banana (200g), chopped coarsely

¼ cup (70g) low-fat yogurt

2 teaspoons honey

2 teaspoons wheatgerm

1 Blend or process all ingredients until smooth.

PER 250ml 0.6g fat; 443kJ (106 cal)

drinks

19

Pulses such as lentils and beans are brain-booster foods that ensure good concentration and improve memory. When buying canned varieties of beans, choose ones low in salt.

baked beetroot salad with cannellini beans, fetta and mint

preparation time 10 minutes (plus standing time) **cooking time** 50 minutes **serves** 1

¼ cup (50g) dried cannellini beans

1 medium beetroot (175g), diced into 3cm pieces

cooking-oil spray

50g goat's fetta, crumbled

50g mesclun

¼ cup loosely packed fresh mint leaves

APPLE DRESSING

2 tablespoons fresh apple juice

2 teaspoons american mustard

1 Place beans in small bowl, cover with water; stand overnight, drain. Rinse under cold water; drain.
2 Cook beans in small saucepan of boiling water, uncovered, until just tender; drain. Rinse under cold water; drain.
3 Preheat oven to moderately hot (200°C/180°C fan-forced).
4 Place beetroot in small shallow baking dish; spray with oil. Bake, covered, about 20 minutes or until tender.
5 Meanwhile, make apple dressing.
6 Place beans and beetroot in medium bowl with remaining ingredients and dressing; toss gently to combine.

APPLE DRESSING Place all ingredients in screw-top jar; shake well.

TIP Canned cannellini or butter beans can be used in this recipe; drain and rinse canned beans before using.

PER SERVING 10.3g fat; 1417kJ (339 cal)

lunch

potato and salami tortilla

preparation time 15 minutes **cooking time** 30 minutes **serves** 4

800g potatoes, peeled, sliced thinly

1 tablespoon olive oil

1 large brown onion (200g), sliced thinly

200g sliced salami

6 eggs, beaten lightly

300ml cream

4 green onions, sliced thickly

¼ cup (25g) coarsely grated mozzarella

¼ cup (30g) coarsely grated cheddar

1 Boil, steam or microwave potato until just tender; drain.

2 Meanwhile, heat oil in medium frying pan; cook brown onion, stirring, until soft. Add salami; cook, stirring, until crisp. Drain salami mixture on absorbent paper.

3 Whisk eggs in large bowl with cream, green onion and cheeses; stir in potato and salami mixture.

4 Pour mixture into heated lightly oiled medium non-stick frying pan; cook, covered, over low heat about 10 minutes or until tortilla is just set. Carefully invert tortilla onto plate, then slide back into pan; cook, uncovered, about 5 minutes or until cooked through. Serve with salad greens, if desired.

TIP For a lower-fat version, use light cream and omit the cheese.

PER SERVING 69.1g fat; 3595kJ (860 cal)
PER SERVING, LOWER-FAT VERSION 48.8g fat; 2817kJ (674 cal)

lavash wrap

preparation time 15 minutes **serves** 1

1 slice wholemeal lavash

¼ small avocado (50g)

1 teaspoon tahini

½ cup (60g) coarsely grated uncooked beetroot

⅓ cup (50g) coarsely grated uncooked pumpkin

¼ small red capsicum (40g), sliced thinly

40g mushrooms, sliced thinly

¼ small red onion (25g), sliced thinly

1 Spread bread with avocado and tahini.

2 Place remaining ingredients on long side of bread; roll to enclose filling.

PER SERVING 13.4g fat; 1463kJ (350 cal)

lunch

Whole grains such as rye, barley and oats are great stress busters. They are a rich source of fibre and also of vital vitamins needed for lasting energy. Choose from the variety of wholegrain breads available to add many nutritional benefits to a simple sandwich.

open rye sandwich

preparation time 10 minutes **makes** 1

1 teaspoon finely chopped fresh basil

1 teaspoon finely chopped fresh mint

1 tablespoon ricotta

1 slice rye bread (40g)

½ cup loosely packed baby rocket leaves

1 small tomato (90g), sliced thinly

½ lebanese cucumber (65g), sliced thinly

1 tablespoon alfalfa sprouts

1 Combine herbs and cheese in small bowl.

2 Spread cheese mixture on bread; top with remaining ingredients.

PER SANDWICH 3.7g fat; 635kJ (152 cal)

soba salad with seaweed, ginger and vegetables

preparation time 10 minutes **cooking time** 5 minutes **serves** 1

Wakame, a bright green seaweed usually sold in dried form, is used in salads, soups and seasonings. It is available from most Asian food stores.

5g wakame

50g soba

1 lebanese cucumber (130g), seeded, cut into matchsticks

1 small carrot (70g), cut into matchsticks

1 tablespoon toasted sesame seeds

1 green onion, sliced thinly

1cm piece fresh ginger (5g), grated

1 teaspoon sesame oil

2 tablespoons fresh lime juice

1 teaspoon soy sauce

1   Place wakame in small bowl, cover with cold water; stand about 10 minutes or until wakame softens, drain. Discard any hard stems; chop coarsely.

2   Meanwhile, cook soba in small saucepan of boiling water, uncovered, until just tender; drain. Rinse under cold water; drain. Chop soba coarsely.

3   Place wakame and soba in medium bowl with remaining ingredients; toss gently to combine.

PER SERVING 12.2g fat; 1367kJ (327 cal)

spinach, capsicum and fetta pizzas

preparation time 5 minutes **cooking time** 10 minutes **serves** 4

4 wholemeal pitta bread (18cm round)

½ cup (125ml) bottled tomato pasta sauce

2 cups (250g) grated pizza cheese

75g baby spinach leaves

1 medium red capsicum (200g), sliced thinly

100g fetta, crumbled

1 Preheat oven to very hot (240°C/220°C fan-forced).
2 Place pitta bread on oven trays, spread with sauce.
3 Sprinkle half of the pizza cheese over pitta. Top with spinach, capsicum and fetta; sprinkle with remaining pizza cheese.
4 Bake about 10 minutes or until browned.

PER SERVING 21.6g fat; 2179kJ (521 cal)

winter vegetable soup with couscous

preparation time 20 minutes **cooking time** 20 minutes **serves** 4

1 tablespoon olive oil

2 medium brown onions (300g), chopped coarsely

3 trimmed celery stalks (300g), chopped coarsely

1 clove garlic, crushed

1 teaspoon sweet paprika

3 medium potatoes (600g), chopped coarsely

2 large parsnips (700g), chopped coarsely

2 large carrots (360g), chopped coarsely

1½ cups (375ml) chicken stock

1.25 litres (5 cups) water

½ cup (100g) couscous

2 tablespoons coarsely chopped fresh flat-leaf parsley

1 Heat oil in large saucepan; cook onion, celery, garlic and paprika, stirring, until onion softens.
2 Add potato, parsnip, carrot, stock and the water. Bring to a boil then reduce heat; simmer, covered, about 15 minutes or until vegetables are tender.
3 Stir in couscous and parsley; cook, uncovered, 2 minutes or until couscous is tender.

PER SERVING 5.6g fat; 1300kJ (311 cal)

Fish and vegetables contain useful amounts of anti-oxidants, protein and amino acids. They're important for maintaining a steady blood-sugar level; this will help to keep your brain alert and your head clear for tackling work.

niçoise salad

preparation time 15 minutes **cooking time** 10 minutes **serves** 4

200g baby green beans, trimmed

3 medium tomatoes (570g), cut into wedges

4 hard-boiled eggs, quartered

425g can tuna in springwater, drained, flaked

½ cup (80g) drained caperberries, rinsed

½ cup (60g) seeded small black olives

¼ cup firmly packed fresh flat-leaf parsley

440g can whole baby potatoes, rinsed, drained, halved

2 tablespoons olive oil

1 tablespoon lemon juice

2 tablespoons white wine vinegar

1 Boil, steam or microwave beans until just tender; drain. Rinse under cold water; drain.
2 Meanwhile, combine tomato, egg, tuna, caperberries, olives, parsley and potato in large bowl.
3 Combine remaining ingredients in screw-top jar; shake well. Add beans to salad, drizzle with dressing; toss gently to combine.

PER SERVING 17.8g fat; 1493kJ (357 cal)

Superfoods for Exam Success

ham, tomato and avocado bruschetta

preparation time 5 minutes **cooking time** 25 minutes **serves** 1

1 medium egg tomato (75g), halved lengthways

2 teaspoons brown sugar

2 thick slices ciabatta

½ small avocado (100g), sliced thinly

50g shaved ham

1 Preheat oven to moderate (180°C/160°C fan-forced).

2 Place tomato halves, cut-side up, on oven tray; sprinkle with sugar. Cook about 20 minutes.

3 Toast bread until lightly browned both sides; serve topped with avocado, ham and tomato.

PER SERVING 22.8g fat; 1944kJ (465 cal)

pizza supreme jaffle

preparation time 10 minutes **cooking time** 10 minutes **serves** 4

1 tablespoon olive oil

2 cloves garlic, crushed

1 small red onion (100g), sliced thinly

1 small green capsicum (150g), sliced thinly

50g swiss brown mushrooms, sliced thinly

1 long loaf pide

¼ cup (70g) tomato paste

120g hot salami, sliced thinly

80g marinated artichoke hearts, drained, sliced thinly

100g bocconcini, sliced thickly

1 Heat oil in large frying pan; cook garlic and onion, stirring, until onion softens. Add capsicum and mushrooms; cook, stirring, until softened.

2 Preheat jaffle maker or sandwich press. Cut bread crossways into four pieces; split each piece horizontally.

3 Spread paste evenly over four pieces of bread, then top with equal amounts of vegetable mixture, salami, artichoke and cheese. Top with remaining bread pieces.

4 Toast sandwiches in jaffle maker or sandwich press.

TIP If you do not have a jaffle maker or sandwich press, you can make these sandwiches in either a frying pan or your oven.

PER SERVING 27.9g fat, 2728kJ (652 cal)

lunch

33

Soup is a speedily made and very sustaining pick-me-up. Be sure to add pasta or noodles to the mix. These inexpensive items contain slow-release carbohydrates that boost energy.

thai chicken noodle soup

preparation time 5 minutes **cooking time** 2 minutes **serves** 1

175g singapore noodles

1½ cups (375ml) chicken stock

½ cup thinly sliced cooked chicken

1 teaspoon red curry paste

1 green onion, sliced thinly

1 tablespoon coarsely chopped fresh coriander

1   Rinse noodles under hot water; drain.

2   Combine noodles, stock, chicken and paste in medium microwave-safe bowl; cook, uncovered, on HIGH (100%) in microwave oven about 2 minutes or until hot.

3   Serve sprinkled with onion and coriander.

PER SERVING 8.9g fat; 1643kJ (393 cal)

tuna, avocado and bean salad

preparation 15 minutes **serves** 4

300g can red kidney beans, rinsed, drained

250g cherry tomatoes, halved

1 cup loosely packed fresh parsley leaves

½ cup loosely packed fresh coriander leaves

1 medium red onion (170g), sliced thinly

2 x 185g cans tuna in oil

¼ cup (60ml) olive oil

¼ cup (60ml) red wine vinegar

2 small avocados (400g), halved

1   Combine kidney beans, tomatoes, herbs and onion in medium bowl; toss gently to combine.

2   Drain tuna, reserve 2 tablespoons of the oil. Combine reserved tuna oil, olive oil and vinegar in a screw-top jar; shake well.

3   Divide salad and flaked tuna among serving plates. Top with avocado; drizzle with dressing.

PER SERVING 35g fat; 1960kJ (469 cal)

lunch

37

lamb, tabbouleh and hummus on pitta

preparation time 10 minutes **makes** 1

1 pocket pitta

1 tablespoon hummus

¼ cup tabbouleh

50g sliced roast lamb

20g baby rocket leaves

1   Cut pitta in half; separate bread to form a pocket. Spread hummus on inside of each pitta. Place equal amounts of tabbouleh, lamb and rocket inside each pitta.

TIP Buy hummus and tabbouleh already prepared from the delicatessen.

PER PITTA 13.1g fat; 1237kJ (296 cal)

tuna and sweet corn sandwich

preparation time 10 minutes **makes** 1

½ x 185g can tuna in springwater, drained, flaked

2 tablespoons canned corn kernels, rinsed, drained

1 tablespoon mayonnaise

2 slices multigrain bread

¼ lebanese cucumber, sliced thinly

1   Combine tuna, corn and mayonnaise in small bowl.
2   Spread tuna mixture on one slice of bread. Top with cucumber and remaining slice of bread.

PER SANDWICH 9.7g fat; 1379kJ (330 cal)

pea, ricotta, mint and spinach sandwich

preparation time 10 minutes **makes** 3

¾ cup (90g) cooked peas

¾ cup (150g) ricotta

¼ cup (60ml) lemon juice

¼ cup finely chopped fresh mint

6 slices soy and linseed bread

60g baby spinach leaves

1 Lightly crush peas with fork. Combine pea mash with ricotta, juice and mint.

2 Spread a third of the pea mixture on one slice of bread; top with spinach and another slice of bread. Repeat with remaining mixture, bread and spinach.

TIP Make the filling in advance; store in an airtight container in the refrigerator for up to three days.

PER SANDWICH 8.5g fat; 995kJ (238 cal)

egg salad open sandwich

preparation time 10 minutes **makes** 3

5 hard-boiled eggs, chopped finely

2 medium tomatoes (300g), chopped coarsely

¼ cup (75g) mayonnaise

3 slices white bread

60g mesclun

1 Combine egg, tomato and mayonnaise in medium bowl.

2 Top one slice of bread with a third of the mesclun and egg mixture. Repeat with remaining mixture, mesclun and bread slices.

TIP Make the filling in advance; store in an airtight container in the refrigerator for up to three days.

PER SANDWICH 19g fat; 1517kJ (363 cal)

lunch

Brown rice has a delicious nutty flavour; it has a higher nutrient content than white. If you're feeling stressed and unsettled, rice is an easy, soothing food to digest. It contains B vitamins essential for energy metabolism.

italian brown rice salad

preparation time 15 minutes **cooking time** 1 hour **serves** 4

3 cups (750ml) vegetable stock

2 teaspoons olive oil

1 small brown onion (80g), chopped finely

1½ cups (300g) medium-grain brown rice

1 teaspoon finely grated lime rind

⅓ cup (45g) toasted slivered almonds

⅔ cup (100g) sun-dried tomatoes, chopped coarsely

½ cup (60g) seeded black olives, chopped coarsely

½ cup coarsely chopped fresh basil

¼ cup coarsely chopped fresh flat-leaf parsley

LIME AND MUSTARD DRESSING

2 tablespoons lime juice

2 tablespoons white wine vinegar

2 cloves garlic, crushed

2 teaspoons dijon mustard

1   Place stock in medium saucepan. Bring to a boil then reduce heat; simmer, covered.
2   Meanwhile, heat oil in large saucepan; cook onion, stirring, until softened. Add rice and rind; stir to coat rice in onion mixture.
3   Add stock. Bring to a boil then reduce heat; simmer, covered, about 50 minutes or until rice is tender and liquid is absorbed.
4   Make lime and mustard dressing.
5   Add remaining ingredients and dressing to rice mixture in pan; toss gently to combine.
6   Serve salad warm; top with fresh flat-leaf parsley, if desired.

LIME AND MUSTARD DRESSING Place all ingredients in a screw-top jar; shake well to combine.

PER SERVING 3.5g fat; 556kJ (133 cal)

lunch

sweet chilli cream cheese

preparation time 10 minutes **makes** 2 cups

250g cream cheese, softened
½ cup (125ml) sour cream
½ cup (125ml) sweet chilli sauce
¼ cup coarsely chopped fresh coriander

1   Beat cheese, sour cream and sauce in small bowl
    with electric mixer until smooth. Stir in coriander.
TIP Store leftover dip, in airtight container, in refrigerator
    for up to one week.

PER TABLESPOON 5.6g fat; 250kJ (60 cal)

snacks

beetroot dip

preparation time 10 minutes **makes** 2½ cups

850g can sliced beetroot, drained
1 clove garlic, quartered
¼ cup (60g) sour cream
1 tablespoon lemon juice

1   Blend or process ingredients until smooth.
TIP Store leftover dip, in airtight container, in refrigerator
    for up to one week.

PER TABLESPOON 1.3g fat; 86kJ (21 cal)

hummus

preparation time 10 minutes **makes** 1¼ cups

300g can chickpeas, rinsed, drained

1 tablespoon tahini

2 tablespoons lemon juice

1 clove garlic, quartered

2 tablespoons water

¼ cup (60ml) olive oil

1 Blend or process chickpeas, tahini, juice, garlic and water until almost smooth. With motor operating, gradually add oil in a thin steady stream until mixture forms a smooth paste.

TIP Store leftover dip, in airtight container, in refrigerator for up to one week.

PER TABLESPOON 5.6g fat; 263kJ (63 cal)

guacamole

preparation time 10 minutes **makes** 2½ cups

2 medium avocados (500g)

½ small red onion (50g), chopped finely

1 medium egg tomato (75g), seeded, chopped finely

1 tablespoon lime juice

¼ cup coarsely chopped fresh coriander

1 Mash avocados in medium bowl; stir in remaining ingredients.

PER TABLESPOON 4g fat; 157kJ (38 cal)

greek open sandwich

preparation time 10 minutes **makes** 1

1 tablespoon cream cheese

1 tablespoon coarsely chopped seeded kalamata olives

1 slice brown bread

handful baby rocket leaves

1 Combine cheese and olives in small bowl. Spread half of the cheese mixture on the bread; top with rocket. Spoon remaining cheese mixture on top.

PER SANDWICH 5.3g fat; 518kJ (124 cal)

mexican open sandwich

preparation time 10 minutes **makes** 1

½ small avocado (100g)

1 teaspoon lemon juice

2 tablespoons canned refried beans

1 pocket pitta

½ small egg tomato (30g), chopped coarsely

1 teaspoon sour cream

pinch paprika

1 Mash avocado with juice in small bowl.

2 Spread beans over pitta; top with avocado mixture, tomato and sour cream. Sprinkle with paprika.

PER SANDWICH 20.6g fat; 1846kJ (441 cal)

No-cook, easy-to-prepare snacks are a must when time is at a premium. Nut mixes and dips and wraps with a variety of fillings all provide essential nutrients with no fuss.

smoked salmon and avocado rice paper rolls

preparation time 20 minutes **makes** 6

½ green onion

½ small avocado (100g), sliced thinly

1 teaspoon lemon juice

6 x 17cm square rice paper sheets

50g thinly sliced smoked salmon, cut into strips

⅓ cup (15g) alfalfa sprouts

¼ cup firmly packed fresh coriander leaves

1   Cut onion into 10cm pieces; slice pieces thinly lengthways. Place avocado and juice in small bowl; toss gently to combine.

2   Place one sheet of rice paper in medium bowl of warm water until just softened. Lift sheet carefully from water; place it, with corner point facing towards you, on a board covered with a tea towel. Place one onion slice horizontally in centre of rice paper, top with a little of the avocado mixture, salmon, sprouts and coriander. Fold corner point facing you up over filling; roll rice paper sheet to enclose filling, folding in sides after first complete turn of roll. Repeat with remaining rice paper sheets and ingredients.

PER ROLL 2.2g fat; 166kJ (40 cal)

dhal with minted cucumber yogurt

preparation time 20 minutes **cooking time** 25 minutes **serves** 4

2 cups (500ml) water

1 cup (200g) red lentils

½ teaspoon ground turmeric

1 teaspoon black mustard seeds

1 tablespoon peanut oil

2 green onions, sliced thinly

1 fresh small red thai chilli, chopped finely

1 clove garlic, crushed

1 small tomato (130g), seeded, chopped finely

2 teaspoons garam masala

MINTED CUCUMBER YOGURT

1 lebanese cucumber (130g), seeded, chopped finely

½ cup (140g) yogurt

¼ cup loosely packed fresh mint leaves, sliced thinly

2 tablespoons lime juice

1   Combine the water, lentils and turmeric in large saucepan. Bring to a boil then reduce heat; simmer, uncovered, about 15 minutes or until lentils are tender, stirring occasionally.

2   Meanwhile, make minted cucumber yogurt.

3   Cook seeds in large heated frying pan, stirring until fragrant. Add oil, onion, chilli, garlic and tomato; cook, stirring, 5 minutes. Add lentil mixture to pan; stir over low heat until heated through. Remove from heat; stir in garam masala.

4   Serve dhal with minted cucumber yogurt and pappadums, if desired.

MINTED CUCUMBER YOGURT Combine ingredients in small bowl.

TIP Store leftover dhal, in airtight container, in refrigerator for up to one week. Reheat in microwave until just warm.

PER SERVING 13.7g fat; 1923kJ (459 cal)

snacks

49

Nuts provide the body with valuable proteins and are especially useful to those who follow a vegetarian diet. They are one of the best food sources of vitamin E, strengthening the immune system and promoting good health.

asian nut mix

preparation time 10 minutes   **cooking time** 35 minutes (plus cooling time)   **makes** 3 cups

1½ cups (225g) unsalted raw cashews

1½ cups (150g) walnuts

2cm piece fresh ginger (10g), grated

1½ teaspoons sweet chilli sauce

2 cloves garlic, crushed

1 tablespoon salt-reduced soy sauce

1   Preheat oven to moderate (180°C/160°C fan-forced).
2   Place cashews on oven tray. Bake about 15 minutes or until browned lightly; cool.
3   Combine cashews with remaining ingredients in large bowl. Spread nut mixture over greased oven tray. Bake, stirring occasionally, about 20 minutes or until crisp; cool.

TIP   Store leftover nut mix in an airtight container for up to one week.

PER CUP   71.6g fat; 3315kJ (793 cal)

Don't feel guilty about indulging in a little chocolate fix occasionally. Chocolate is one of the best feel-good foods there is and its beneficial properties as a mood enhancer should far outweigh any concerns you may have about its calorie content.

chocolate nut clusters

preparation time 20 minutes (plus refrigeration time) **cooking time** 5 minutes **makes** 24

150g milk eating chocolate, chopped coarsely

¼ cup (35g) toasted shelled unsalted pistachios

¼ cup (35g) toasted slivered almonds

½ cup (80g) sultanas

1   Line oven tray with baking paper.
2   Place chocolate in small heatproof bowl; place bowl over small saucepan of simmering water, stirring until chocolate melts. Stir in nuts and sultanas.
3   Drop heaped teaspoonfuls of chocolate mixture onto prepared tray. Refrigerate, uncovered, until chocolate is set.

TIPS Store nut clusters in an airtight container for up to one week. Chocolate nuts clusters can also be made with carob.

PER CLUSTER 3.2g fat; 248kJ (59 cal)

chocolate wheaties

preparation time 25 minutes **cooking time** 12 minutes **makes** 35

90g butter

½ cup (100g) firmly packed brown sugar

1 egg, beaten lightly

¼ cup (20g) desiccated coconut

¼ cup (25g) wheatgerm

¾ cup (120g) wholemeal plain flour

½ cup (75g) white self-raising flour

150g dark eating chocolate, melted

1   Preheat oven to moderate (180°C/160°C fan-forced).

2   Beat butter and sugar in small bowl with electric mixer until smooth; add egg, beat until combined.

3   Stir in coconut, wheatgerm and flours. Roll rounded teaspoons of mixture into balls, place about 3cm apart on lightly greased oven trays; flatten with a fork.

4   Bake about 12 minutes or until lightly browned. Cool on trays.

5   Dip half of each biscuit in chocolate; leave to set on wire racks.

TIP   Store biscuits in an airtight container for up to one week.

PER BISCUIT 4.5g fat; 342kJ (82 cal)

Blueberries are a true superfood. They help prevent heart disease and may combat ageing. They're an excellent source of dietary fibre and anti-oxidants. Frozen blueberries are just as nutritious as fresh ones and are cheaper, too.

blueberry scones

preparation time 10 minutes   **cooking time** 20 minutes   **makes** 8

2 cups (300g) self-raising flour

2 tablespoons icing sugar mixture

1¼ cups (310ml) buttermilk

150g blueberries

1   Preheat oven to hot (220°C/200°C fan-forced). Grease shallow 20cm-round sandwich pan.

2   Sift flour and icing sugar into large bowl; pour in enough buttermilk to mix to a sticky dough. Fold in blueberries.

3   Gently knead dough on lightly floured surface until just smooth; use hand to flatten out dough to about a 3cm thickness. Cut eight x 5.5cm rounds from dough; place rounds, slightly touching, in prepared pan. Bake, uncovered, about 20 minutes or until browned lightly; turn scones onto wire rack.

4   Serves scones with vanilla yogurt, if desired.

PER SCONE   2.6g fat; 832kJ (199 cal)

citrus poppy seed muffins

preparation time 15 minutes **cooking time** 20 minutes **makes** 12

125g butter, softened

2 teaspoons finely grated lemon rind

2 teaspoons finely grated orange rind

⅔ cup (150g) caster sugar

2 eggs, beaten lightly

2 cups (300g) self-raising flour

½ cup (250ml) milk

2 tablespoons poppy seeds

1 medium orange (240g)

icing sugar mixture, for dusting

1 Preheat oven to moderately hot (200°C/180°C fan-forced). Grease 12-hole (⅓-cup/80ml) muffin pan.

2 Combine butter, rinds, caster sugar, egg, sifted flour and milk in medium bowl; beat with electric mixer until just combined. Increase speed to medium; beat until mixture is just changed in colour; stir in poppy seeds.

3 Divide mixture among holes of prepared pan; bake muffins, uncovered, about 20 minutes. Stand muffins in pan for a few minutes before turning onto wire rack.

4 Peel rind thinly from orange, avoiding any white pith. Cut rind into thin strips. To serve, dust muffins with icing sugar mixture and top with orange strips.

TIP Store muffins in an airtight container for up to one week.

PER MUFFIN 11.4g fat; 1041kJ (249 cal)

cheese, corn and bacon muffins

preparation time 20 minutes (plus standing time) **cooking time** 25 minutes **makes** 12

½ cup (85g) polenta

½ cup (125ml) milk

3 bacon rashers (210g), rind removed, chopped finely

4 green onions, chopped finely

1½ cups (225g) self-raising flour

1 tablespoon caster sugar

310g can corn kernels, drained

125g can creamed corn

100g butter, melted

2 eggs, beaten lightly

50g piece cheddar cheese

¼ cup (30g) coarsely grated cheddar

1 Preheat oven to moderately hot (200°C/180°C fan-forced). Oil 12-hole (⅓-cup/80ml) muffin pan.

2 Mix polenta and milk in small bowl, cover; stand 20 minutes.

3 Meanwhile, cook bacon, stirring, in heated small non-stick frying pan for 2 minutes. Add onion to pan; cook, stirring, for another 2 minutes. Remove pan from heat; cool bacon mixture about 5 minutes.

4 Sift flour and sugar into large bowl; stir in corn kernels, creamed corn and bacon mixture. Add melted butter, eggs and polenta mixture; mix muffin batter only until just combined.

5 Spoon 1 tablespoon of the batter into each hole of prepared muffin pan. Cut piece of cheese into 12 equal pieces; place one piece in the centre of each muffin pan hole. Divide remaining batter among muffin pan holes; sprinkle grated cheese over each. Bake muffins, uncovered, about 20 minutes. Turn muffins onto wire rack. Serve muffins warm.

TIP Store muffins in an airtight container for up to one week.

PER MUFFIN 12.2g fat; 1018kJ (243 cal)

snacks

Omega-3 fatty acids are vital in promoting good health. Because we cannot manufacture them ourselves, eating foods rich in these essential fatty acids is important. Fish and seafood are the best sources. Aim to eat at least one portion a week.

roasted mediterranean-style fish and vegetables

preparation time 5 minutes **cooking time** 25 minutes **serves** 4

2 x 440g cans whole baby potatoes, drained, rinsed

250g cherry tomatoes

1 whole garlic bulb, separated into unpeeled cloves

2 large red onions (600g), chopped coarsely

3 rosemary sprigs, chopped coarsely

¼ cup (60ml) olive oil

8 x 75g skinless bream fillets

¼ cup (60ml) lemon juice

¼ cup firmly packed fresh basil leaves

1   Preheat oven to hot (220°C/200°C fan-forced).
2   Place potatoes and tomatoes in large lightly oiled baking dish; crush slightly with potato masher. Sprinkle garlic, onion and rosemary into baking dish; drizzle with half of the oil.
3   Roast the vegetables, uncovered, for 15 minutes. Place fish on vegetables, sprinkle with juice and remaining oil; bake, uncovered, about 10 minutes or until fish is cooked as desired. Sprinkle with basil leaves.

PER SERVING 22.1g fat; 1931kJ (461 cal)

mains

steamed asian bream

preparation time 10 minutes **cooking time** 15 minutes **serves** 1

1 whole bream (240g)

3cm piece fresh ginger (15g), cut into matchsticks

1 green onion, sliced thinly

1 small carrot (70g), cut into matchsticks

1 tablespoon soy sauce

1 teaspoon sesame oil

1   Preheat oven to moderately hot (200°C/180°C fan-forced).

2   Lightly oil sheet of foil large enough to enclose fish. Place fish on foil, fill cavity with half of the vegetables. Brush fish with combined soy sauce and oil; top with remaining vegetables.

3   Fold edges of foil to enclose fish; place fish parcel on oven tray. Cook about 15 minutes or until fish is cooked as desired.

4   Serve fish sprinkled with fresh coriander leaves, if desired.

PER SERVING 11.2g fat; 357kJ (229 cal)

The grill and barbecue are a busy person's best friend. Simple meals can be prepared without the used of added fats. Flavours and nutrients are retained with this healthy cooking method.

grilled tuna with red cabbage salad

preparation time 15 minutes **cooking time** 10 minutes **serves** 4

1 tablespoon olive oil

1 medium red onion (170g), sliced thinly

2 cups (160g) finely shredded red cabbage

2 cups (160g) finely shredded chinese cabbage

¼ cup (60ml) cider vinegar

1 large green apple (200g), sliced thinly

1 cup loosely packed fresh flat-leaf parsley leaves

4 x 200g tuna steaks

1 Heat oil in wok or large frying pan; stir-fry onion and cabbages 2 minutes. Add vinegar; bring to a boil. Boil 1 minute. Remove from heat; stir in apple and parsley.

2 Meanwhile, cook fish on heated lightly oiled grill plate (or grill or barbecue) until cooked as desired. Serve fish with warm cabbage salad.

PER SERVING 16.2g fat; 1635kJ (391 cal)

fish and snow pea green curry

preparation time 30 minutes **cooking time** 15 minutes **serves** 4

1¼ cups (250g) jasmine rice

2 teaspoons peanut oil

1 medium brown onion (150g), chopped finely

3 small green chillies, seeded, sliced thinly

¼ cup (75g) green curry paste

1⅔ cups (400ml) coconut milk

4 x 200g firm white fish fillets, skinned, chopped coarsely

200g snow peas, halved

4 green onions, sliced thinly

¼ cup coarsely chopped fresh coriander

1 Cook rice in large saucepan of boiling water, uncovered, until tender; drain. Cover to keep warm.

2 Meanwhile, heat oil in large saucepan; cook brown onion, chilli and paste, stirring, until onion softens. Stir in coconut milk; bring to a boil. Add fish, reduce heat; simmer, uncovered, 5 minutes. Add snow peas and green onion; stir gently until vegetables are just tender. Remove from heat; stir in half of the coriander. Serve curry with rice; sprinkle with remaining coriander.

PER SERVING 27.9g fat; 2839kJ (678 cal)

chicken tandoori pockets with raita

preparation time 10 minutes **cooking time** 10 minutes **makes** 8

1 tablespoon lime juice

⅓ cup (100g) tandoori paste

¼ cup (70g) yogurt

400g chicken tenderloins

8 large flour tortillas

60g snow pea tendrils

RAITA

1 cup (280g) yogurt

1 lebanese cucumber (130g), halved, seeded, chopped finely

1 tablespoon finely chopped fresh mint

1　Combine juice, paste and yogurt in medium bowl; add chicken, toss to coat chicken in marinade.

2　Cook chicken, in batches, on heated oiled grill plate (or grill or barbecue) until cooked through. Stand 5 minutes; slice thickly.

3　Meanwhile, make raita. Heat tortillas according to manufacturer's instructions.

4　Place equal amounts of chicken, tendrils and raita on a quarter section of each tortilla; fold tortilla in half, then in half again to enclose filling and form triangle-shaped pockets.

RAITA Combine ingredients in small bowl.

PER POCKET 8.8g fat; 1003kJ (240 cal)

mains

71

Poultry is higher in protein and lower in saturated fats than red meats. It contains tryptophan, an essential amino acid that may help ease depression and insomnia. Avoid eating the skin because it is high in fat.

grilled chicken with barley pilaf

preparation time 10 minutes **cooking time** 55 minutes **serves** 4

1 cup (215g) pearl barley

2 cups (500ml) water

2 cups (500ml) chicken stock

250g cherry tomatoes

150g yellow teardrop tomatoes

4 single chicken breast fillets (680g)

½ teaspoon coarsely ground black pepper

½ cup coarsely chopped fresh basil

2 green onions, sliced thinly

1 tablespoon dijon mustard

1 Preheat oven to hot (220°C/200°C fan-forced).

2 Cook barley with the water and stock in medium saucepan, uncovered, over low heat, about 50 minutes or until most of the liquid is absorbed, stirring occasionally.

3 Meanwhile, roast tomatoes on oven tray lined with baking paper, uncovered, about 20 minutes or until just browned and softened.

4 Cook chicken on heated lightly oiled grill plate (or grill or barbecue) until cooked through.

5 Stir tomatoes, pepper, basil and onion into barley. Serve chicken, dolloped with mustard, with barley pilaf.

PER SERVING 11.3g fat; 1726kJ (412 cal)

clay pot chicken

preparation time 10 minutes (plus refrigeration time) **cooking time** 1 hour **serves** 4

4 cloves garlic, crushed

1 tablespoon fish sauce

2 tablespoons soy sauce

2 tablespoons lime juice

10cm stick fresh lemon grass (20g), chopped finely

800g chicken thigh fillets, halved

1 large brown onion (200g), quartered

1 fresh long red chilli, sliced thinly

½ cup (125ml) chicken stock

100g fresh shiitake mushrooms, halved

4 green onions, cut into 4cm pieces

½ small cabbage (600g), cut into 6cm squares

1   Combine garlic, sauces, juice and lemon grass in large bowl, add chicken; toss chicken to coat in marinade. Cover; refrigerate 3 hours or overnight.
2   Preheat oven to moderate (180°C/160°C fan-forced).
3   Place chicken mixture in clay pot or 2.5-litre (10-cup) ovenproof dish with brown onion, chilli and stock; mix gently to combine. Cook, covered, 45 minutes. Add mushroom, green onion and cabbage to dish; cook, covered, stirring occasionally, about 15 minutes or until chicken is cooked.

PER SERVING 14.9g fat; 1484kJ (355 cal)

chicken and fresh pea risoni

preparation time 15 minutes **cooking time** 30 minutes **serves** 4

400g chicken breast fillets

1 litre (4 cups) chicken stock

300g sugar snap peas, trimmed

1 cup (120g) frozen peas

1 tablespoon olive oil

1 small leek (200g), sliced thinly

1 clove garlic, crushed

500g risoni

½ cup (125ml) dry white wine

1 tablespoon white wine vinegar

1 tablespoon finely chopped fresh tarragon

1   Combine chicken and stock in medium frying pan. Bring to a boil then reduce heat; simmer, uncovered, about 10 minutes or until cooked through. Cool chicken in poaching liquid 10 minutes. Remove chicken from pan; reserve stock. Slice chicken thinly.

2   Meanwhile, boil, steam or microwave peas separately, until just tender; drain.

3   Heat oil in large saucepan; cook leek and garlic, stirring, until leek softens. Add risoni; stir to coat in leek mixture. Add wine; stir until wine is almost absorbed. Add reserved stock. Bring to a boil then reduce heat; simmer, uncovered, stirring occasionally, until stock is absorbed and risoni is tender. Stir in vinegar; remove from heat. Gently stir in chicken, peas and tarragon.

PER SERVING 9.7g fat; 2862kJ (684 cal)

Research indicates that a lack of iron in the diet can have a detrimental effect on memory. Lamb is rich in iron and an excellent food for those studying. Excess fat is easily visible and can be trimmed off before cooking.

lamb and lentil curry

preparation time 15 minutes **cooking time** 55 minutes **serves** 4

1 cup (200g) yellow split peas

1 tablespoon olive oil

600g lamb fillets, diced into 4cm pieces

2 large brown onions (400g), sliced thinly

5cm piece fresh ginger (25g), chopped finely

2 cloves garlic, crushed

2 tablespoons ground coriander

1 tablespoon sweet paprika

½ teaspoon cayenne pepper

200g yogurt

2 medium tomatoes (300g), chopped coarsely

1¾ cups (430ml) chicken stock

⅔ cup (160ml) light coconut cream

150g baby spinach leaves

⅓ cup coarsely chopped fresh coriander

1 Cook split peas in medium saucepan of boiling water, uncovered, until just tender; drain.

2 Meanwhile, heat half of the oil in large saucepan; cook lamb, in batches, stirring, until cooked as desired. Drain on absorbent paper.

3 Heat remaining oil in same pan; cook onion, stirring, about 15 minutes or until caramelised. Add ginger, garlic, ground coriander, paprika and cayenne; cook, stirring, until fragrant. Add yogurt; cook 5 minutes, without boiling, stirring occasionally.

4 Add tomato, stock and coconut cream. Bring to a boil then reduce heat; simmer, uncovered, about 15 minutes or until sauce thickens slightly.

5 Return lamb to pan with split peas and spinach; cook, stirring, until heated through. Remove from heat; stir in fresh coriander.

PER SERVING 19.3g fat; 2153kJ (515 cal)

spicy sausage and couscous salad

preparation time 15 minutes **cooking time** 10 minutes **serves** 4

500g spicy beef sausages

1½ cups (375ml) beef stock

1½ cups (300g) couscous

20g butter

1 tablespoon finely grated lemon rind

¾ cup coarsely chopped fresh flat-leaf parsley

120g baby rocket leaves

⅓ cup (50g) toasted pine nuts

2 fresh red thai chillies, seeded, sliced thinly

1 small red onion (100g), sliced thinly

1 clove garlic, crushed

⅓ cup (80ml) lemon juice

2 tablespoons olive oil

1. Cook sausages on heated grill plate (or grill or barbecue) until browned and cooked through. Drain on absorbent paper; slice thickly.
2. Meanwhile, bring stock to a boil in medium saucepan. Remove from heat; stir in couscous and butter. Cover; stand about 10 minutes or until liquid is absorbed, fluffing couscous with fork occasionally.
3. Place sausage and couscous in large bowl with remaining ingredients; toss gently to combine.

PER SERVING 45g fat; 3621kJ (865 cal)

vietnamese beef, chicken and tofu soup

preparation time 20 minutes **cooking time** 1 hour 5 minutes **serves** 4

3 litres (12 cups) water

500g gravy beef

1 star anise

2.5cm piece fresh galangal (15g), halved

¼ cup (60ml) soy sauce

2 tablespoons fish sauce

340g chicken breast fillets

1½ cups (120g) bean sprouts

1 cup loosely packed fresh coriander leaves

4 green onions, sliced thinly

2 fresh red thai chillies, sliced thinly

⅓ cup (80ml) lime juice

300g firm tofu, diced into 2cm pieces

1 Combine the water, beef, star anise, galangal and sauces in large saucepan. Bring to a boil then reduce heat; simmer, covered, 30 minutes. Uncover; simmer 20 minutes. Add chicken; simmer, uncovered, 10 minutes.

2 Combine sprouts, coriander, onion, chilli and juice in medium bowl.

3 Remove beef and chicken from pan; reserve stock. Discard fat and sinew from beef; slice thinly. Slice chicken thinly. Return beef and chicken to pan, then reheat soup.

4 Divide tofu among serving bowls; ladle hot soup over tofu, sprinkle with sprout mixture. Serve with lime wedges and extra chilli, if desired.

PER SERVING 18.8g fat; 1410kJ (337 cal)

mains

Beef contains immune-boosting nutrients and is a good source of high-quality protein. Eaten in moderation and trimmed of excess fat, it is a nutritious and versatile ingredient that gives the body's defences a boost when under stress.

beef, barley and mushroom stew

preparation time 35 minutes **cooking time** 2 hours 20 minutes **serves** 4

1kg beef chuck steak, diced into 3cm pieces

¼ cup (35g) plain flour

2 tablespoons olive oil

20g butter

2 medium brown onions (300g), chopped finely

3 cloves garlic, crushed

1 medium carrot (120g), chopped finely

1 trimmed celery stalk (100g), chopped finely

4 sprigs fresh thyme

1 bay leaf

½ cup (100g) pearl barley

2 cups (500ml) beef stock

½ cup (125ml) dry white wine

2 cups (500ml) water

200g swiss brown mushrooms, quartered

200g button mushrooms, quartered

1 Preheat oven to moderately slow (160°C/140°C fan-forced).
2 Coat beef in flour; shake off excess. Heat oil in large flameproof casserole dish; cook beef, in batches, until browned all over.
3 Melt butter in same dish; cook onion, garlic, carrot, celery and herbs, stirring, until vegetables soften. Add barley, stock, wine and the water; bring to a boil. Return beef to dish, cover; cook 1½ hours.
4 Stir in mushrooms; cook, uncovered, about 30 minutes or until beef and mushrooms are tender.
5 Serve stew with mashed potato and sprinkled with fresh thyme, if desired.

PER SERVING 25.9g fat; 2646kJ (633 cal)

stir-fried beef, bok choy and gai larn

preparation time 10 minutes **cooking time** 25 minutes **serves** 4

2 tablespoons peanut oil

500g beef strips

2 cloves garlic, crushed

2cm piece fresh ginger (10g), grated

1 tablespoon finely chopped fresh lemon grass

2 fresh red thai chillies, seeded, sliced thinly

1kg baby bok choy, chopped coarsely

500g gai larn, chopped coarsely

4 green onions, sliced thinly

2 tablespoons kecap manis

1 tablespoon fish sauce

¼ cup (60ml) sweet chilli sauce

¼ cup coarsely chopped fresh coriander

1 Heat half of the oil in wok or large frying pan; stir-fry beef, in batches, until browned all over.

2 Heat remaining oil in same wok; stir-fry garlic, ginger, lemon grass and chilli until fragrant. Add vegetables; stir-fry until vegetables just wilt. Return beef to wok with remaining ingredients; stir-fry until heated through. Serve with rice, if desired.

PER SERVING 17.6g fat; 1434kJ (343 cal)

mains

rigatoni bolognese

preparation time 5 minutes **cooking time** 30 minutes **serves** 4

1 medium brown onion (150g), chopped coarsely

1 small carrot (70g) chopped coarsely

1 trimmed celery stalk (100g), chopped coarsely

2 tablespoons olive oil

2 cloves garlic, crushed

500g beef mince

2 tablespoons tomato paste

¾ cup (180ml) beef stock

425g can crushed tomatoes

2 tablespoons finely chopped fresh basil

500g rigatoni

¼ cup (20g) coarsely grated parmesan

1 Blend or process onion, carrot and celery until chopped finely.

2 Heat oil in large saucepan, cook onion mixture and garlic, stirring occasionally, 5 minutes.

3 Add mince to pan; cook, stirring, until browned lightly.

4 Stir in paste, stock and undrained tomatoes. Bring to a boil then reduce heat; simmer, uncovered, about 20 minutes or until bolognese thickens. Stir in basil.

5 Meanwhile, cook pasta in large saucepan of boiling water, uncovered, until just tender; drain.

6 Serve pasta topped with bolognese; sprinkle with cheese and, if desired, freshly ground black pepper.

PER SERVING 21.2g fat; 3185kJ (762 cal)

Lentils help to stave off hunger and provide a steady supply of energy. They are high in fibre, which helps to lower cholesterol levels, and are packed with minerals, vitamins and protein.

lentil and bean burger

preparation time 20 minutes **cooking time** 25 minutes (plus refrigeration time) **serves** 4

1 cup (200g) red lentils

420g can four-bean mix, rinsed, drained

1 egg

4 green onions, chopped coarsely

2 tablespoons coarsely chopped fresh coriander

4 hamburger buns

¾ cup (195g) bottled tomato salsa

8 butter lettuce leaves

40g bean sprouts

40g snow pea sprouts, trimmed

1 lebanese cucumber (130g), sliced thinly

1 Cook lentils in medium saucepan of boiling water, uncovered, until tender; drain. Cool 10 minutes.

2 Blend or process lentils, beans and egg until mixture forms a smooth paste. Combine in medium bowl with onion and coriander; cover, refrigerate 1 hour.

3 Using floured hands, shape lentil mixture into four patties; cook patties in heated lightly oiled large non-stick frying pan until browned both sides and heated through. Remove from pan; cover to keep warm.

4 Split buns in half; toast cut-sides of buns. Spread buns with half the salsa; sandwich lettuce, sprouts, cucumber, patties and remaining salsa between buns.

PER SERVING 5.5g fat; 2006kJ (480 cal)

rice and chickpea salad

preparation time 15 minutes **cooking time** 10 minutes (plus standing and refrigeration time) **serves** 6

1 cup (200g) white long-grain rice

2 cups (500ml) water

300g can chickpeas, rinsed, drained

¼ cup (40g) sultanas

¼ cup (35g) dried apricots, chopped finely

2 green onions, sliced thinly

2 tablespoons toasted pine nuts

BALSAMIC ORANGE DRESSING

1 teaspoon finely grated orange rind

⅓ cup (80ml) orange juice

1 tablespoon balsamic vinegar

1 clove garlic, crushed

1cm piece fresh ginger (5g), grated

1   Combine rice and the water in medium heavy-based saucepan. Bring to a boil then reduce heat; simmer, covered, about 8 minutes or until rice is tender. Remove from heat; stand, covered, 10 minutes. Fluff rice with fork; cool then refrigerate, covered, until cold.

2   Meanwhile, make dressing.

3   Combine rice with remaining ingredients in large bowl; add balsamic orange dressing, toss gently to combine.

BALSAMIC ORANGE DRESSING Combine all ingredients in screw-topped jar; shake well.

PER SERVING 4.3g fat; 929kJ (222 cal)

oven-roasted ratatouille with almond gremolata

preparation time 10 minutes **cooking time** 40 minutes **serves** 1

2 baby eggplants (120g), chopped coarsely

1 medium zucchini (120g), chopped coarsely

1 small red capsicum (150g), chopped coarsely

1 clove garlic, crushed

2 teaspoons olive oil

100g mushrooms, chopped coarsely

125g cherry tomatoes, halved

ALMOND GREMOLATA

2 tablespoons coarsely chopped fresh flat-leaf parsley

2 tablespoons coarsely chopped fresh basil

1 teaspoon finely grated lemon rind

2 tablespoons toasted slivered almonds, chopped coarsely

1 clove garlic, crushed

1 Preheat oven to moderately hot (200°C/180°C fan-forced).

2 Combine eggplant, zucchini, capsicum, garlic and oil in small shallow baking dish. Roast, uncovered, 30 minutes, stirring occasionally. Add mushroom and tomato; roast, uncovered, about 10 minutes or until vegetables are just tender.

3 Meanwhile, combine ingredients for almond gremolata in small bowl.

4 Serve ratatouille topped with gremolata.

PER SERVING 21.6g fat; 1304kJ (312 cal)

mains

Low in kilojoules and rich in vitamins, tomatoes are a handy, inexpensive, year-round food that is very versatile in cooking. Store ripe tomatoes at room temperature, not in the refrigerator, to help retain their flavour and texture.

fresh tomato and chilli pasta

preparation time 10 minutes **cooking time** 15 minutes **serves** 4

500g penne

⅓ cup (80ml) olive oil

2 teaspoons bottled crushed garlic

2 teaspoons bottled chopped chilli

4 medium ripe tomatoes (800g), chopped

1 cup chopped fresh flat-leaf parsley

½ cup (40g) parmesan flakes

1   Cook pasta in large saucepan of boiling water, uncovered, until just tender; drain.

2   Meanwhile, heat oil in large frying pan, add garlic and chilli; cook, stirring, about 1 minute or until fragrant. Add tomato and parsley; remove from heat.

3   Add sauce mixture to pasta; toss gently. Serve topped with cheese.

PER SERVING 19.9g fat; 2547kJ (608 cal)

fruit skewers with honey yogurt

preparation time 30 minutes **cooking time** 10 minutes **serves** 2

You need six 20cm wooden skewers for this recipe; soak them in cold water before using to prevent them from splintering and scorching during cooking.

½ small pineapple (450g)

1 large orange (300g)

125g strawberries

1 large banana (230g)

15g butter

2 tablespoons firmly packed brown sugar

2 teaspoons lemon juice

½ cup (140g) honey yogurt

1 Peel pineapple half; cut away and discard core. Cut pineapple into 3cm pieces. Peel orange thickly to remove pith; separate orange segments. Remove hulls from strawberries; cut in half crossways. Peel banana; cut into 3cm slices.

2 Thread fruit, alternating varieties, onto skewers; place on oven tray.

3 Combine butter, sugar and juice in small saucepan over low heat, stirring until sugar dissolves. Pour butter mixture over skewers, making sure all fruits are coated in mixture.

4 Cook skewers, in batches, on heated lightly greased grill plate (or grill or barbecue) about 5 minutes or until browned lightly. Serve skewers with yogurt.

PER SERVING 8.5g fat; 1352kJ (323 cal)

desserts

Pears can be eaten as a healthy snack, sliced onto cereal or a salad or cooked as a dessert. They contain pectin, a soluble fibre that helps regulate blood cholesterol levels.

pears in coffee syrup

preparation time 10 minutes **cooking time** 20 minutes **serves** 2

½ cup (110g) caster sugar

2 cups (500ml) water

2 medium pears (460g), peeled

2 teaspoons instant coffee granules

1   Combine sugar and the water in medium saucepan; stir over low heat until sugar is dissolved. Add pears. Bring to a boil then reduce heat; simmer, covered, about 15 minutes or until pears are soft.

2   Remove pears from syrup. Return syrup to a boil, then reduce heat; simmer, uncovered, about 10 minutes or until syrup reduces to about 1 cup (250ml).

3   Combine syrup with coffee in small jug; serve pears with coffee syrup and, if desired, chopped dark chocolate and vanilla ice-cream.

PER SERVING 0.2g fat; 1296kJ (310 cal)

rice pudding with raspberries

preparation time 10 minutes **cooking time** 1 hour 20 minutes **serves** 2

¼ cup (50g) white short-grain rice

1½ cups (375ml) milk

½ teaspoon vanilla extract

2 tablespoons caster sugar

RASPBERRY COMPOTE

150g frozen raspberries

2 teaspoons caster sugar

1   Preheat oven to moderately slow (170°C/150°C fan-forced).

2   Rinse rice well under cold water; drain. Spread rice over bottom of shallow 1-litre (4-cup) baking dish.

3   Combine milk, extract and sugar in small saucepan; bring to a boil. Pour hot milk mixture carefully over rice in baking dish; mix gently with fork. Cover dish tightly with foil; bake about 1 hour 15 minutes or until rice softens and almost all liquid is absorbed.

4   Meanwhile, make raspberry compote.

5   Serve rice pudding topped with raspberry compote.

RASPBERRY COMPOTE Combine ingredients in small saucepan; stir over low heat until sugar dissolves. Cool 10 minutes.

PER SERVING 5.4g fat; 1237kJ (296 cal)

grilled bananas with Malibu syrup

preparation time 10 minutes **cooking time** 5 minutes **serves** 2

Malibu is the brand name of a rum-based coconut liqueur.

2 large ripe bananas (460g)

2 tablespoons maple syrup

1 tablespoon Malibu

2 tablespoons toasted shredded coconut

1   Split bananas lengthways. Combine maple syrup and liqueur; brush about a quarter of the mixture over cut-sides of bananas.

2   Cook bananas, cut-side down, on heated lightly oiled grill plate (or grill or barbecue) until lightly browned and heated through.

3   Serve bananas while hot, drizzled with warmed remaining syrup, toasted coconut and whipped cream, if desired.

PER SERVING 2.7g fat; 1122kJ (268 cal)

Some recipes are naughty but very nice. When you're preparing for exams or an all-important interview, treats can be helpful to your sense of wellbeing. A balanced diet is one that offers all things in moderation.

ice-cream with choc-peanut sauce

preparation time 5 minutes **cooking time** 10 minutes (plus standing time) **serves** 2

60g Snickers chocolate bar, chopped coarsely

¼ cup (60ml) cream

1 tablespoon coffee-flavoured liqueur

500ml (2 cups) vanilla ice-cream

1 Place Snickers and cream in small saucepan; cook, stirring, without boiling, until Snickers melts and sauce thickens slightly. Remove from heat.

2 Stir in liqueur; stand 5 minutes before serving drizzled over scoops of ice-cream.

PER SERVING 48.7g fat; 3152kJ (753 cal)

caramelised apple tarts

preparation time 15 minutes cooking time 20 minutes serves 4

1 sheet ready-rolled puff pastry

1 egg yolk

1 tablespoon milk

1 tablespoon caster sugar

2 large apples (400g)

60g butter, softened

⅓ cup (75g) firmly packed brown sugar

½ teaspoon ground cinnamon

1 Preheat oven to hot (220°C/200°C fan-forced). Lightly grease oven tray.

2 Score pastry in crosshatch pattern with sharp knife. Brush pastry with combined yolk and milk; sprinkle with caster sugar. Cut into four squares; place on prepared tray.

3 Cut unpeeled apples crossways in 5mm slices. Place sliced apples, overlapping if necessary, over base of large baking dish; dot with butter, sprinkle with brown sugar and cinnamon. Bake pastry and apple slices, uncovered, about 10 minutes or until pastry is puffed and browned. Remove pastry from oven. Turn apple slices; bake, uncovered, about 10 minutes or until soft and browned.

4 Top pastry with apple; drizzle with caramel mixture in baking dish. Serve with frozen vanilla yogurt or ice-cream, if desired.

PER SERVING 23.5g fat; 1751kJ (419 cal)

desserts

summer berry sundae

preparation time 5 minutes **cooking time** 5 minutes **serves** 1

1 tablespoon caster sugar

125g frozen mixed berries

1 teaspoon finely grated orange rind

250ml (1 cup) vanilla ice-cream

2 tablespoons toasted macadamias, chopped coarsely

1   Stir sugar and berries in small saucepan over heat, without boiling, until sugar dissolves. Bring to a boil then reduce heat; simmer, uncovered, about 2 minutes or until berries soften. Stir in rind; cool 10 minutes.

2   Layer ice-cream, berry mixture and nuts into serving glass.

PER SERVING 32.9g fat; 2257kJ (540 cal)

blackberry soufflés

preparation time 15 minutes (plus refrigeration time) **cooking time** 20 minutes **serves** 4

300g frozen blackberries

1 tablespoon water

⅓ cup (75g) caster sugar

4 egg whites

1 tablespoon icing sugar mixture

1 Preheat oven to moderately hot (200°C/180°C fan-forced).

2 Combine blackberries and the water in small saucepan. Bring to a boil then reduce heat; simmer, uncovered, until blackberries soften. Add caster sugar; stir over medium heat, without boiling, until sugar dissolves. Bring to a boil then reduce heat; simmer, uncovered, 5 minutes. Remove from heat; using the back of a large spoon, push blackberry mixture through sieve into small bowl, discarding seeds in sieve. Refrigerate 15 minutes.

3 Beat egg whites in medium bowl with electric mixer until soft peaks form. Fold in blackberry mixture until combined.

4 Divide mixture among four lightly greased 1-cup (250ml) ovenproof dishes; place on tray. Bake, uncovered, about 12 minutes or until soufflés are puffed and browned lightly. Dust with sifted icing sugar mixture; serve immediately.

PER SERVING 0.2g fat; 526kJ (126 cal)

desserts

Yogurt can be used as a topping for breakfast cereals and desserts, in dips and sauces and as a quick-fix snack. It is easily digested by people who are lactose intolerant and is an excellent source of calcium and protein.

rhubarb and muesli parfait

preparation time 10 minutes **cooking time** 5 minutes **serves** 1

1 cup (110g) rhubarb, chopped coarsely

2 tablespoons firmly packed brown sugar

⅓ cup (95g) greek yogurt

⅓ cup (45g) toasted muesli

1 Combine rhubarb and sugar in small, shallow microwave-safe dish.

2 Cook, covered, in a single layer, on HIGH (100%) about 3 minutes or until tender; drain if necessary. Cool.

3 Place rhubarb in ¾-cup capacity serving dish. Top with yogurt and muesli.

PER SERVING 11.3g fat; 1735kJ (415 cal)

ARTICHOKES

globe large flower-bud of a member of the thistle family, having tough petal-like leaves; edible in part when cooked.

hearts tender centre of the globe artichoke. Artichoke hearts can be harvested fresh from the plant or purchased in brine canned or in glass jars.

BEANS

black an earthy-flavoured dried bean also known as turtle beans or black kidney beans.

black-eyed also known as black-eyed peas, are the dried seed of a variant of the snake or yard bean.

borlotti also known as roman beans, they can be eaten fresh or dried. Are a pale pink or beige colour with darker red spots.

cannellini small white bean available canned and dried. Used in baked beans and in traditional ham and bean soup.

sprouts also known as bean shoots; tender new growths of assorted beans and seeds germinated for consumption as sprouts.

BEETROOT

also known as red beets or just beets; a firm, round root vegetable.

BOK CHOY

also known as bak choy, pak choy or chinese white cabbage; has a mild mustard taste. Use both stems and leaves. *Baby bok choy* is smaller and more tender, and often cooked whole.

BREADS

chapati a popular unleavened Indian bread, chapati is used to scoop up pieces of food in lieu of cutlery. Made from whole-wheat flour, salt and water, and dry-fried on a tawa (a cast-iron griddle). Available from Indian food stores and supermarkets.

ciabatta the word means 'slipper' in Italian, which is the traditional shape of this popular crisp-crusted white bread.

lavash flat, unleavened bread of Mediterranean origin; good as a wrapper or torn up and used for dips.

pide also known as Turkish bread, comes in long (about 45cm) flat loaves as well as individual rounds. Made from wheat flour and sprinkled with sesame or black onion seeds.

pitta a slightly leavened, soft, flat bread that puffs up when baked, leaving a hollow 'pocket' that can be stuffed with savoury fillings or pulled apart and used for scooping up dips. Sold in large, flat pieces that separate into two thin rounds and in smaller, thick pieces (pocket pitta). A wholemeal variety is also available.

sourdough so-named, not because it is sour in taste, but because it's made by using a small amount of 'starter dough', which contains a yeast culture, mixed into flour and water. Part of the resulting dough is saved to be used as the starter dough next time.

tortilla thin, round unleavened bread originating in Mexico. Made from either wheat flour or corn.

BURGHUL

also known as bulghur wheat; hulled steamed wheat kernels that, once dried, are crushed into various size grains. Not the same as cracked wheat. Used in Middle-Eastern dishes such as kibbeh and tabbouleh.

BUTTERMILK

originally the liquid left after cream was separated from milk, today it is commercially made similarly to yogurt.

CAPSICUM

also known as bell pepper or pepper. Discard seeds and membranes before use.

CARAWAY SEEDS

a member of the parsley family, available in seed or ground form.

CARDAMOM

native to India; can be purchased in pod, seed or ground form. Has a distinctive aromatic, sweetly rich flavour, and is one of the world's most expensive spices.

CHEESE

fetta crumbly goat- or sheep-milk cheese with a sharp, salty taste.

mozzarella soft, spun-curd cheese traditionally made from water-buffalo milk.

ricotta soft, white, cow-milk cheese. Is a sweet, moist cheese with a slightly grainy texture and a fat content of around 8.5%.

romano a hard cheese made from cow or sheep milk. Straw-coloured and grainy in texture, it is mainly used for grating. Parmesan can be substituted.

parmesan also known as parmigiano, parmesan is a hard, grainy cow-milk cheese.

CHICKPEAS

also called channa, garbanzos or hummus; a sandy-coloured, irregularly spherical legume. It is frequently used in Mediterranean cooking.

CHILLI

cayenne pepper a thin-fleshed, long, extremely hot, dried red chilli, usually purchased ground; both arbol and guajillo chillies are the fresh sources for cayenne.

chipotle chillies hot, dried, smoked jalapeños.

jalapeños fairly hot, green chillies, available bottled in brine or fresh from specialty greengrocers.

thai red small, medium hot, and bright red in colour.

CHINESE CABBAGE

also known as peking cabbage, wong bok or petsai. Elongated in shape with pale green, crinkly leaves.

CINNAMON

available both in the piece (called sticks or quills) and ground into powder; one of the world's most common spices, it is used universally as a sweet, fragrant flavouring for both sweet and savoury foods.

CORIANDER

also known as cilantro or chinese parsley; bright-green-leafed herb with a

Glossary

pungent flavour. Both stems and roots are used in Thai cooking.

COUSCOUS a fine, grain-like cereal product, originally from North Africa; made from semolina.

EGGPLANT also known as aubergine; ranging in size from tiny to very large and in colour from pale green to deep purple, eggplant has an equally wide variety of flavours.

FENNEL also known as finocchio or anise; can be eaten raw or braised or fried. Also the name given to dried seeds having a licorice flavour.

FIVE-SPICE POWDER a fragrant mixture of ground cinnamon, cloves, star anise, sichuan pepper and fennel seeds.

GAI LARN also known as chinese kale or chinese broccoli; appreciated more for its stems than its coarse leaves.

GARAM MASALA a blend of roasted, ground spices, including cardamom, cinnamon, cloves, coriander, fennel and cumin. Black pepper and chilli can be added for a hotter version.

GINGER
fresh also known as green or root ginger; the thick gnarled root of a tropical plant.
ground also known as powdered ginger; cannot be substituted for fresh ginger.
pickled pink pickled paper-thin shavings of ginger in a mixture of vinegar, sugar and natural colouring.

HUMMUS a Middle Eastern salad or dip made from softened dried chickpeas, garlic, lemon juice and tahini; it is available ready-made from delicatessens and supermarkets.

KAFFIR LIME LEAVES also known as bai magrood; look like two glossy, dark green leaves joined end to end, forming an hourglass shape. Sold fresh, dried or frozen; the dried leaves are less potent so double the number if you substitute them for fresh leaves. A strip of fresh lime peel may be substituted for each kaffir lime leaf..

MAPLE SYRUP a thick syrup distilled from the sap of the maple tree. Maple-flavoured syrup or pancake syrup is not an adequate substitute.

MESCLUN a salad mixture or gourmet salad mix which is a combination of assorted young lettuce and other green leaves, including baby spinach leaves, mizuna and curly endive.

MUSHROOMS
flat large, flat mushrooms with a rich earthy flavour, they are ideal for filling with other ingredients and for barbecuing. They are sometimes misnamed field mushrooms, which are, in fact, wild mushrooms.
shiitake when fresh are also known as chinese black, forest or golden oak mushrooms; are large and meaty and have the earthiness and taste of wild mushrooms. When dried, they are known as donko or dried chinese mushrooms; rehydrate before use.
swiss brown light to dark brown mushrooms with full-bodied flavour.

MUSTARD
american a sweet, bright yellow mustard that contains mustard seeds, garlic, sugar and spices. Serve with hamburgers.
dijon pale brown, creamy, fairly mild French mustard.
english a hot, pungent, deep yellow mustard. Serve with roast beef and ham.
wholegrain also known as seeded mustard. A French-style, coarse-grain mustard made from crushed mustard seeds and dijon-style French mustard. Works well with cold meats.

NOODLES
soba made from buckwheat flour, these Japanese noodles are available frozen and dried.
fresh egg noodles also known as ba mee or yellow noodles. Range in size from very fine strands to wide, thick spaghetti-like pieces as thick as a shoelace.
fresh rice also known as ho fun, khao pun, sen yau, pho or kway tiau. Purchased in various widths or large sheets, which are cut into the desired width. Chewy and pure white, they do not need pre-cooking before use.

ONIONS
green also known as scallion or, incorrectly, shallot; an immature onion picked before the bulb has formed, having a long, bright-green edible stalk.
red also known as spanish, red spanish or bermuda onion; a sweet-flavoured, large, purple-red onion.

PANCETTA an Italian unsmoked bacon; pork belly is cured in salt and spices, rolled into a sausage shape and then dried for several weeks. Use sliced or chopped as an ingredient, rather than eating it on its own.

PAPRIKA ground, dried red capsicum (bell pepper), available sweet or hot.

PARSLEY, FLAT-LEAF also known as continental or italian parsley.

PEARL BARLEY barley that has had its outer husk (bran) removed, and been steamed and polished before being used in cooking.

POLENTA a flour-like cereal made of ground corn (maize); similar to cornmeal but finer and lighter in colour; also the name of the dish made from it.

RICE PAPER SQUARES softened in hot water, used as a wrapper for fresh vegetables, prawns and suchlike, to make an uncooked spring roll; generally served at room temperature. Made from ground rice, flour, salt and water; imported from South-East Asia and sold packaged in square or round pieces.

ROLLED OATS flattened oat grain rolled into flakes and traditionally used for porridge. Instant oats are also available, but use traditional oats for baking.

STAR ANISE a dried star-shaped fruit of a tree native to China. The pods, which have an astringent aniseed or licorice flavour, are widely used in the Asian kitchen. Available whole or ground, it is an essential ingredient in five-spice powder.

TAHINI a rich sesame seed paste sold at delicatessens and Middle Eastern food stores; most often used in hummus, baba ghanoush and other Lebanese-style recipes.

TOFU also known as bean curd, tofu is a bland, slightly nutty food made from soy bean 'milk'. Its neutral taste gives it the ability to absorb the flavours of the food with which it is cooked. Available from supermarkets in water-packed containers. Once opened, store in the refrigerator, in water, for just a few days.

TORTILLAS thin, round unleavened bread originating from Mexico; can easily be made at home or purchased frozen, fresh or vacuum-packed. Two kinds are available, one made from wheat flour and the other from corn.

WAKAME a deep green, edible seaweed popular in Japan. Has the fresh taste of the sea; used in soups and in simmered dishes. Wakame comes in fresh and dried forms from Asian grocery shops. Soften dried wakame in cold water; cook briefly.

Glossary

117

Index

MEASURES

One Australian metric measuring cup holds approximately 250ml; one Australian metric tablespoon holds 20ml; one Australian metric teaspoon holds 5ml.

The difference between one country's measuring cups and another's is within a two- or three-teaspoon variance, and will not affect your cooking results. North America, New Zealand and the United Kingdom use a 15ml tablespoon.

All cup and spoon measurements are level. The most accurate way of measuring dry ingredients is to weigh them. When measuring liquids, use a clear glass or plastic jug with the metric markings.

We use large eggs with an average weight of 60g.

DRY MEASURES

METRIC	IMPERIAL
15g	½oz
30g	1oz
60g	2oz
90g	3oz
125g	4oz (¼lb)
155g	5oz
185g	6oz
220g	7oz
250g	8oz (½lb)
280g	9oz
315g	10oz
345g	11oz
375g	12oz (¾lb)
410g	13oz
440g	14oz
470g	15oz
500g	16oz (1lb)
750g	24oz (1½lb)
1kg	32oz (2lb)

LIQUID MEASURES

METRIC	IMPERIAL
30ml	1 fluid oz
60ml	2 fluid oz
100ml	3 fluid oz
125ml	4 fluid oz
150ml	5 fluid oz (¼ pint/1 gill)
190ml	6 fluid oz
250ml	8 fluid oz
300ml	10 fluid oz (½ pint)
500ml	16 fluid oz
600ml	20 fluid oz (1 pint)
1000ml (1 litre)	1¾ pints

LENGTH MEASURES

METRIC	IMPERIAL
3mm	⅛in
6mm	¼in
1cm	½in
2cm	¾in
2.5cm	1in
5cm	2in
6cm	2½in
8cm	3in
10cm	4in
13cm	5in
15cm	6in
18cm	7in
20cm	8in
23cm	9in
25cm	10in
28cm	11in
30cm	12in (1ft)

OVEN TEMPERATURES

These oven temperatures are only a guide for conventional ovens.
For fan-forced ovens, check the manufacturer's manual.

	°C (CELSIUS)	°F (FAHRENHEIT)	GAS MARK
Very slow	120	250	½
Slow	150	275-300	1-2
Moderately slow	170	325	3
Moderate	180	350-375	4-5
Moderately hot	200	400	6
Hot	220	425-450	7-8
Very hot	240	475	9

Conversion Chart

ARE YOU MISSING SOME OF THE WORLD'S FAVOURITE COOKBOOKS?

The Australian Women's Weekly Cookbooks are available from bookshops, cookshops, supermarkets and other stores all over the world. You can also buy direct from the publisher, using the order form below.

TITLE	RRP	QTY	TITLE	RRP	QTY
Asian, Meals in Minutes	£6.99		Japanese Cooking Class	£6.99	
Babies & Toddlers Good Food	£6.99		Kids' Birthday Cakes	£6.99	
Barbecue Meals In Minutes	£6.99		Kids Cooking	£6.99	
Beginners Cooking Class	£6.99		Lean Food	£6.99	
Beginners Simple Meals	£6.99		Low-carb, Low-fat	£6.99	
Beginners Thai	£6.99		Low-fat Feasts	£6.99	
Best Food	£6.99		Low-fat Food For Life	£6.99	
Best Food Desserts	£6.99		Low-fat Meals in Minutes	£6.99	
Best Food Fast	£6.99		Main Course Salads	£6.99	
Best Food Mains	£6.99		Mexican	£6.99	
Cakes Biscuits & Slices	£6.99		Middle Eastern Cooking Class	£6.99	
Cakes Cooking Class	£6.99		Midweek Meals in Minutes	£6.99	
Caribbean Cooking	£6.99		Muffins, Scones & Breads	£6.99	
Casseroles	£6.99		New Casseroles	£6.99	
Chicken	£6.99		New Classics	£6.99	
Chicken Meals in Minutes	£6.99		New Finger Food	£6.99	
Chinese Cooking Class	£6.99		New Salads (Oct 06)	£6.99	
Christmas Cooking	£6.99		Party Food and Drink	£6.99	
Chocolate	£6.99		Pasta Meals in Minutes	£6.99	
Cocktails	£6.99		Potatoes	£6.99	
Cooking for Friends	£6.99		Salads: Simple, Fast & Fresh	£6.99	
Detox	£6.99		Saucery	£6.99	
Dinner Beef	£6.99		Sauces Salsas & Dressings	£6.99	
Dinner Lamb	£6.99		Sensational Stir-Fries	£6.99	
Dinner Seafood	£6.99		Short-order Cook	£6.99	
Easy Australian Style	£6.99		Slim	£6.99	
Easy Curry	£6.99		Stir-fry	£6.99	
Easy Spanish-Style	£6.99		Superfoods for Exam Success	£6.99	
Essential Soup	£6.99		Sweet Old Fashioned Favourites	£6.99	
French Food, New	£6.99		Tapas Mezze Antipasto & other bites	£6.99	
Fresh Food for Babies & Toddlers	£6.99		Thai Cooking Class	£6.99	
Get Real, Make a Meal	£6.99		Traditional Italian	£6.99	
Good Food Fast	£6.99		Vegetarian Meals in Minutes	£6.99	
Great Lamb Cookbook	£6.99		Vegie Food	£6.99	
Greek Cooking Class	£6.99		Weekend Cook	£6.99	
Grills	£6.99		Wicked Sweet Indulgences	£6.99	
Healthy Heart Cookbook	£6.99		Wok, Meals in Minutes	£6.99	
Indian Cooking Class	£6.99		TOTAL COST:	£	

Mr/Mrs/Ms _____

Address _____

_____ Postcode _____

Day time phone _____ Email* (optional) _____

I enclose my cheque/money order for £ _____

or please charge £ _____

to my: ☐ Access ☐ Mastercard ☐ Visa ☐ Diners Club

PLEASE NOTE: WE DO NOT ACCEPT SWITCH OR ELECTRON CARDS

Card number | | | | | | | | | | | | | | | | |

Expiry date _____ 3 digit security code *(found on reverse of card)* _____

Cardholder's name_____ Signature _____

To order: Mail or fax – photocopy or complete the order form above, and send your credit card details or cheque payable to: Australian Consolidated Press (UK), Moulton Park Business Centre, Red House Road, Moulton Park, Northampton NN3 6AQ, phone (+44) (0) 1604 497531 fax (+44) (0) 1604 497533, e-mail books@acpmedia.co.uk or order online at www.acpuk.com
Non-UK residents: We accept the credit cards listed on the coupon, or cheques, drafts or International Money Orders payable in sterling and drawn on a UK bank. Credit card charges are at the exchange rate current at the time of payment.
Postage and packing UK: Add £1.00 per order plus 50p per book.
Postage and packing overseas: Add £2.00 per order plus £1.00 per book.
All pricing current at time of going to press and subject to change/availability.
Offer ends 31.12.2007

* By including your email address, you consent to receipt of any email regarding this magazine, and other emails which inform you of ACP's other publications, products, services and events, and to promote third party goods and services you may be interested in.